ANXIOUS GENERATION

Practical Tools for Managing and unravelling the Modern Epidemic of Stress and Anxiety in the Digital Age

Belingo Aknel

Dedication

To all those who have faced the silent battles of anxiety, this book is for you.

To the families and friends who provide unwavering support and understanding, your love and compassion are the lifelines that keep us grounded.

To the therapists, counsellors, and mental health professionals who dedicate their lives to guiding others through their darkest moments, your work changes lives.

To the communities, both online and offline, that offer a sense of belonging and solidarity, your existence is a beacon of hope.

And to the readers, may this book serve as a reminder that you are not alone, and that together, we can navigate the complexities of anxiety and emerge stronger.

With heartfelt gratitude,

Belingo Aknel

Copyright

Legal Notice and Disclaimer

All content in "The Anxious Generation," is for informational purposes only. This book is not intended to be a substitute for professional medical advice, diagnosis, or treatment. Always seek the advice of your physician or other qualified health provider with any questions you may have regarding a medical condition.

The author and publisher of this book have made every effort to ensure that the information contained herein is accurate and up-to-date at the time of publication. However, medical knowledge and practice can change over time, and the author and publisher do not guarantee that the information in this book is complete, correct, or current. This book is not intended to provide medical advice or to be used as a substitute for the care and guidance of a licensed healthcare professional. The information provided is for educational purposes only and should not be used to diagnose or treat any mental health condition.

Readers are strongly encouraged to seek the advice of a qualified mental health professional before making any changes to their treatment or lifestyle. Do not disregard professional medical advice

By using this book, you acknowledge that you have read, understood, and agreed to the terms and conditions of this legal notice and disclaimer.

Thank you for your understanding and cooperation.

Table of Content

Introduction

As we sit on the transition point of cultural directions, it seems easier to understand and, therefore, empathize with the growing sense of anxiety that seems increasingly prevalent today. And indeed, it is prevalent – recent studies have shown that more than half of university students have suffered distress to the level that they have difficulty with work or are in too much pain to sleep. The World Health Organization lists depression as the fourth-ranked affliction worldwide, and the World Mental Health

Survey indicates that over 15% of the world's population have clinical depression or anxiety disorders. Mental Health America's depression screening has shown a 45% increase in tests specifically for anxiety over the last year.

Some have even called our current societal problem with anxiety an epidemic, and it is difficult to argue with the suggestion given our fragile and deprecating treatment of that which is actually within our control.

Part 1: The Meaning of Anxious Generation

The anxious generation is the second generation in the digital age. The digital age is defined as the social changes and technological advancements that took place from the 1970s to the early 1990s. These societal norms and enhanced technical tools laid the foundation for the expansion of technology. The evolution of this technology has led the way to the digital generation. This generation is naturally distinct from previous outside generations, as they were the first to truly adopt and infuse technology into their everyday lives at a mere eight years old. The impact of technology on each successive generation is remarkable. The transcript documents the life and times of the first digital generation from 2000 to 2020.

In 2017, a direct focus on the people and their behavior brought about the discovery of something different. They were found to still be withdrawn from society and physically present but mentally removed. These impressive, tired souls observing the environment but still lost in cyberspace became identified as the anxious generation.

The anxious generation sees no difference as noise levels reach a deafening 100 decibels. The breaking news is not believable, and the entertainment and information are an artificial reality transmitted from a digital world. There are 87.4 taxonomies, stereotypes, and stigmas including the label "anxious generation" that have been allocated to Generation Z. All mold them through behavioral actions or collective identities as individuals. Each expert's understanding is both illusion and the loss of a personal identity.

Despite all that is known, something is wrong. What is it?

Part 2: Understanding the Anxiety

Chapter 1 delves into the multifaceted nature of anxiety, providing a foundational understanding necessary for comprehending the broader discussions in the book. It begins by examining the neurobiological mechanisms underpinning anxiety. Anxiety is rooted in the brain's response to perceived threats, primarily involving the amygdala, which plays a key role in processing fear. When the amygdala perceives a threat, it triggers the release of stress hormones like cortisol and adrenaline, preparing the body for a fight-or-flight response. This evolutionary mechanism, designed to protect us from immediate dangers, becomes problematic when activated too frequently or without real danger, leading to chronic anxiety.

The chapter also explores the historical evolution of anxiety as a concept. In ancient times, anxiety was often seen through a spiritual or supernatural lens, with symptoms attributed to demonic possession or divine punishment. As medical knowledge advanced, particularly during the Enlightenment, anxiety began to be understood more as a psychological and physiological condition. Early medical texts started to describe symptoms and suggest treatments, although these were rudimentary compared to modern standards. The 19th and 20th centuries saw significant advancements, with figures like Sigmund Freud contributing to the understanding of anxiety through psychoanalytic theory, and later, the development of behavioral and cognitive-behavioral approaches.

Different types of anxiety disorders are then outlined, providing clarity on what constitutes clinical anxiety. Generalized Anxiety Disorder (GAD) is characterized by persistent and excessive worry about various aspects of life, such as health, work, or social interactions. Individuals with GAD often find it difficult to control their worry and experience physical symptoms like restlessness, fatigue, and muscle tension. Panic Disorder involves recurrent panic attacks, which are sudden episodes of intense fear accompanied by physical symptoms like palpitations, sweating, and shortness of breath. These attacks can occur unexpectedly and can be so severe that they are often mistaken for heart attacks.

Social Anxiety Disorder, another common type of anxiety, involves a profound fear of social situations where one might be judged or scrutinized by others. This fear can lead to avoidance of social interactions and significant distress in situations that cannot be avoided. People with social anxiety may worry excessively about being embarrassed or humiliated in front of others, leading to symptoms like blushing, sweating, and difficulty speaking. Specific phobias involve an intense fear of a particular object or situation, such as heights, spiders, or flying. The fear is disproportionate to the actual danger posed and can lead to avoidance behavior that impacts daily functioning.

Understanding these different disorders is crucial for recognizing the diverse ways in which anxiety can manifest and affect individuals. Each type of anxiety disorder has unique characteristics and requires tailored approaches to treatment and management. This section emphasizes the importance of proper diagnosis and the role of mental health professionals in identifying and addressing these conditions.

The chapter also touches on the psychological and environmental factors that contribute to anxiety. Psychological factors include personality traits such as neuroticism, which predispose individuals to experience negative emotions more intensely. Early childhood experiences, such as trauma or neglect, can also increase the risk of developing anxiety disorders later in life. Environmental factors include stressors such as financial difficulties, relationship problems, and work-related stress. These stressors can trigger or exacerbate anxiety symptoms, particularly in individuals who are already predisposed to anxiety.

In addition to exploring the causes of anxiety, the chapter discusses the impact of anxiety on daily life. Anxiety can significantly impair an individual's ability to function in various areas, including work, school, and social interactions. Chronic anxiety can lead to physical health problems, such as cardiovascular disease and gastrointestinal issues, due to the prolonged activation of the body's stress response. It can also affect sleep, leading to insomnia and further exacerbating anxiety symptoms. The social impact of anxiety is also significant, as individuals may avoid social situations, leading to isolation and loneliness.

Chapter 1 concludes by highlighting the importance of addressing anxiety from a comprehensive perspective. This includes understanding the biological, psychological, and environmental factors that contribute to anxiety, as well as recognizing the diverse ways in which anxiety can manifest. By providing a detailed foundation of what anxiety is, how it develops, and how it affects individuals, this chapter sets the stage for the subsequent discussions on cultural influences, specific demographics, coping mechanisms, and the role of community

support

Part 3: Cultural and Societal Influences

This chapter explores the various cultural and societal factors that contribute to the rising levels of anxiety in modern society. One of the most significant influences is social media. With the rapid growth and ubiquity of platforms like Facebook, Instagram, Twitter, and Tik-Tok, social media has become an integral part of daily life, especially for younger generations. The constant use of these platforms has profound effects on mental health, primarily through mechanisms such as social comparison, cyberbullying, and the fear of missing out (FOMO).

Social media fosters a culture of comparison. Users often present idealized versions of their lives, showcasing achievements, vacations, and curated moments that may not reflect reality. This creates a benchmark against which others measure their own lives, often unfavorably. Constant exposure to these idealized portrayals can lead to feelings of inadequacy, low self-esteem, and increased anxiety, as individuals struggle to match the perceived perfection of their peers. The concept of FOMO further exacerbates these feelings, as users are continually reminded of events and experiences they are not part of, leading to a sense of exclusion and anxiety about missing out on life's opportunities.

Cyberbullying is another detrimental aspect of social media that significantly impacts mental health. Unlike traditional bullying, cyberbullying can be relentless and pervasive, following individuals into their homes through their devices. The anonymity provided by the internet can embolden perpetrators and intensify the harassment. Victims of cyberbullying often experience heightened levels of anxiety, depression, and, in severe cases, suicidal ideation. The constant connectivity and visibility on social media make it difficult for individuals to escape from negative interactions, contributing to sustained emotional distress.

Economic instability is another critical factor contributing to the rise of anxiety. In today's fast-paced and competitive world, economic pressures are pervasive. Job insecurity, stagnant wages, and rising costs of living create a stressful environment where financial concerns are a constant source of anxiety. For many, the fear of losing a job, struggling to pay bills, or not being able to afford basic necessities is a significant stressor. The gig economy and freelance work, while offering flexibility, also come with the unpredictability of income and lack of job security, further contributing to financial anxiety.

The burden of student debt is a significant source of anxiety for young adults. As higher education costs continue to rise, many graduates find themselves saddled with substantial debt, which can take decades to repay. This financial strain impacts their ability to achieve traditional milestones such as buying a home, starting a family, or saving for retirement, perpetuating a cycle of anxiety and stress. Additionally, the pressure to succeed academically and professionally in a competitive job market adds to the anxiety experienced by this demographic.

Political uncertainty and global issues also play a substantial role in the rise of anxiety. The current political climate is characterized by polarization, instability, and frequent changes in policies that directly affect people's lives. Issues such as immigration, healthcare, and climate change are sources of significant concern for many individuals. The 24-hour news cycle and constant exposure to media coverage of political conflicts and global crises can exacerbate feelings of helplessness and anxiety. The unpredictable nature of political events and the potential for drastic changes in governance contribute to a sense of instability and fear about the future.

Global issues like climate change, pandemics, and geopolitical tensions add another layer of anxiety. The existential threat posed by climate change, with its potential to cause widespread environmental, economic, and social disruptions, is a source of chronic anxiety for many, particularly younger generations who will face the long-term consequences. The COVID-19 pandemic highlighted the vulnerabilities in global health systems and economies, leading to widespread uncertainty and anxiety about health, safety, and economic stability.

In summary, Chapter 2 of "The Anxious Generation" explores how cultural and societal factors such as social media, economic pressures, and political uncertainty contribute to the rising levels of anxiety in modern society. Social media fosters a culture of comparison, cyberbullying, and FOMO, all of which negatively impact mental health. Economic instability, driven by job insecurity, financial pressures, and student debt, creates a stressful environment that perpetuates anxiety. Political uncertainty and global issues add to this sense of instability, creating a climate where anxiety is increasingly prevalent. By understanding these factors, we can begin to address the root causes of anxiety and work towards creating a more supportive and resilient society.

Part 4: The Youth Epidemic

The Youth Epidemic addresses the alarming rise in anxiety among young people, a demographic particularly vulnerable to mental health issues. Understanding the factors contributing to this increase and the unique challenges faced by this age group is essential for several reasons:

The importance

1. **Early Intervention**: Addressing anxiety in youth can prevent the development of more

severe mental health issues later in life. Early intervention can significantly improve long-term outcomes by equipping young people with the tools and coping mechanisms needed to manage anxiety effectively.

2. **Developmental Impact**: Adolescence and young adulthood are critical periods for emotional and psychological development. Anxiety during these formative years can interfere with key developmental milestones, such as forming healthy

relationships, achieving academic success, and developing a stable sense of identity.

3. **Educational Implications**: Anxiety can severely impact academic performance, leading to decreased concentration, absenteeism, and lower grades. Understanding the causes and consequences of anxiety in students can help educators create supportive environments that enhance learning and reduce stress.

4. **Social and Emotional Well-being:** Anxiety in young people can lead to social

isolation, difficulty in forming and maintaining friendships, and a decreased sense of well-being. This chapter highlights the importance of fostering supportive social networks and teaching emotional regulation skills to mitigate these effects.

5. **Long-term Societal Impact**: The mental health of today's youth will shape the future of society. Addressing the anxiety epidemic in young people is critical for creating a resilient and productive future workforce and society. By investing in the mental health of young people, we can ensure a

healthier, more stable society in the long run.

The Consequences

Failure to address the rise of anxiety in youth can have significant and far-reaching consequences:

Chronic Mental Health Issues: If left untreated, anxiety can lead to chronic mental health conditions such as depression, substance abuse, and other anxiety disorders. These conditions can persist into adulthood, affecting all aspects of an individual's life.

Educational and Career Setbacks: Anxiety can lead to academic underachievement, dropping out of school, and difficulty in pursuing higher education or stable employment. This can result in a cycle of underemployment and financial instability, further exacerbating mental health issues.

Physical Health Problems: Chronic anxiety is associated with a range of physical health problems, including cardiovascular disease, gastrointestinal issues, and weakened immune function. Young people experiencing high levels of anxiety are at greater risk of developing these health issues over time.

Social Isolation and Relationship Difficulties: Anxiety can lead to social withdrawal, making it difficult for young people to form and maintain healthy relationships. This can result in feelings of loneliness and isolation, which can further worsen anxiety and lead to a diminished quality of life.

Increased Risk of Suicide: Anxiety, particularly when combined with depression, significantly increases the risk of suicidal thoughts and behaviors. The youth suicide rate has been rising, making it imperative to address anxiety and its contributing factors to prevent tragic outcomes.

Economic Costs: The economic burden of untreated anxiety includes healthcare costs, lost productivity, and decreased educational and professional attainment. Addressing anxiety in youth can reduce these costs and contribute to a healthier, more productive society.

Part 5: Understanding Anxiety in Adulthood

As a therapist, I have worked with many people over many years who have suffered from varying degrees of anxiety and all of its subsequent angst. Although anxiety symptoms appeared across all adult age groups coming for help for difficulties in their lives, there was often also an increasing presence of anxiety within the younger adult age groups who were presenting at my consulting rooms. All of these adults wished to utilize the best methods to overcome their difficulties, and I worked with many who achieved their goals. They were clearly enriched by the whole therapeutic process. However, many people continue to view therapists with a degree of suspicion, and so often it is the person who prefers to gain an understanding of their distress within their own personal life structure, which results in this type of search.

Relevance of Anxiety in Adulthood

Anxiety in adulthood is a significant public health concern with wide-ranging implications for individuals, families, workplaces, and society at large. Understanding its relevance is crucial for several reasons:

Prevalence and Impact: Anxiety disorders are among the most common mental health conditions in adults, affecting millions worldwide. Their prevalence and the profound impact on daily functioning and quality of life make them a critical area of focus.

Economic and Workplace Implications: Adults with anxiety disorders often face challenges in the workplace, including decreased productivity, absenteeism, and difficulty maintaining employment. This has broader economic implications due to lost productivity and increased healthcare costs.

Physical Health Correlations: Chronic anxiety is linked to various physical health issues, including cardiovascular diseases, gastrointestinal problems, and weakened immune function. Understanding these connections highlights the importance of addressing anxiety to improve overall health outcomes.

Family and Relationship Dynamics: Anxiety in adults can strain relationships and family dynamics, affecting parenting, marital satisfaction, and social interactions. Addressing anxiety can lead to healthier family environments and better social support systems.

Mental Health Comorbidities: Anxiety often coexists with other mental health conditions such as depression, substance abuse, and post-traumatic stress disorder (PTSD). A comprehensive understanding of anxiety can facilitate more effective treatment and management of these comorbid conditions.

Effects of Anxiety in Adulthood

Anxiety in adulthood can manifest in various ways, significantly affecting different aspects of life. Here are the key areas impacted by anxiety in adults:

Personal and Emotional Well-being: Chronic anxiety can lead to persistent feelings of worry, fear, and unease. Adults may experience difficulty concentrating, irritability, and restlessness. These emotional disturbances can reduce overall life satisfaction and well-being.

Physical Health: Anxiety triggers the body's stress response, leading to increased levels of stress hormones like cortisol and adrenaline. Prolonged exposure to these hormones can result in physical health problems, including hypertension, heart disease, and gastrointestinal disorders. Anxiety can also disrupt sleep patterns, leading to insomnia and further exacerbating physical health issues.

Workplace Performance: Adults with anxiety may struggle with concentration, decision-making, and time management at work. This can lead to decreased productivity, missed deadlines, and errors. Additionally, anxiety-related absenteeism can result in job instability and reduced career advancement opportunities. Workplace anxiety can also impact interpersonal relationships with colleagues and supervisors, leading to increased stress and job dissatisfaction.

Social Relationships: Anxiety can cause adults to withdraw from social interactions, leading to isolation and loneliness. Fear of social situations, known as social anxiety disorder, can prevent individuals from forming and maintaining relationships, attending social events, or engaging in activities they once enjoyed. This social withdrawal can further exacerbate feelings of loneliness and depression.

Family and Parenting: Anxiety can significantly impact family dynamics. Adults with anxiety may struggle with parenting responsibilities, leading to inconsistent or overprotective parenting styles. This can affect children's emotional and psychological development. Additionally, anxiety can strain marital relationships, leading to communication difficulties, conflicts, and decreased marital satisfaction.

Financial Stability: The economic impact of anxiety includes increased healthcare costs for treatment and medication, as well as potential loss of income due to decreased work performance or job loss. Financial stress can exacerbate anxiety, creating a cycle of economic instability and mental health decline.

Substance Abuse and Dependency: Some adults may turn to alcohol, drugs, or other substances as a coping mechanism for anxiety. This can lead to substance abuse and dependency, which further complicates mental health issues and introduces additional health risks. The interplay between anxiety and substance abuse can create a challenging cycle that requires comprehensive treatment approaches.

Chronic Mental Health Conditions: Untreated anxiety can lead to the development of chronic mental health conditions. For example, persistent anxiety can increase the risk of developing major depressive disorder. The co-occurrence of anxiety and depression, known as comorbidity, can complicate diagnosis and treatment, making it more challenging to manage both conditions effectively.

In summary, "The Anxious Generation" emphasizes the profound relevance and effects of anxiety in adulthood. Anxiety is highly prevalent among adults and has far-reaching implications for personal well-being, physical health, workplace performance, social relationships, family dynamics, financial stability, substance abuse, and chronic mental health conditions. Recognizing and addressing anxiety in adults is critical for improving individual health outcomes, enhancing workplace productivity, fostering healthier relationships, and reducing the economic burden on society. By understanding the multifaceted impact of anxiety, we can develop more effective strategies for prevention, intervention, and support for adults struggling with this pervasive mental health issue.

Part 6: The Future of Anxiety

This explores various coping mechanisms and therapeutic approaches that individuals can use to manage and reduce anxiety. This chapter aims to provide practical strategies and insights into different treatments that have been shown to be effective. Understanding these methods is crucial for both individuals suffering from anxiety and mental health professionals seeking to offer the best care possible.

Cognitive-Behavioral Therapy (CBT)

CBT is one of the most widely used and researched forms of psychotherapy for anxiety disorders. It is based on the premise that negative thought patterns and behaviors contribute to anxiety, and by changing these patterns, individuals can reduce their anxiety levels.

Cognitive Restructuring: This involves identifying and challenging negative thoughts that contribute to anxiety. Therapists help patients recognize irrational or distorted thinking and replace these thoughts with more realistic and positive ones. For example, if someone has a fear of public speaking, they may learn to replace thoughts of "I'll embarrass myself" with "I am prepared and can handle this."

Exposure Therapy: Exposure therapy is a component of CBT where individuals are gradually and systematically exposed to the situations or objects they fear. This helps them build tolerance and reduce the anxiety response over time. For instance, someone with a phobia of heights might start by looking at pictures of tall buildings and gradually work up to standing on a balcony.

Behavioral Activation: This technique encourages individuals to engage in activities that they have been avoiding due to anxiety. By participating in these activities, individuals can break the cycle of avoidance and inactivity, which often exacerbates anxiety. Engaging in positive activities can improve mood and reduce anxiety symptoms.

Mindfulness and Meditation:

Mindfulness and meditation practices have gained popularity as effective tools for managing anxiety. These practices focus on being present in the moment and accepting thoughts and feelings without judgment.

Mindfulness-Based Stress Reduction (MBSR): MBSR is an eight-week program that combines mindfulness meditation and yoga to help individuals manage stress and anxiety. Participants learn techniques such as body scans, mindful breathing, and mindful movement. Studies have shown that MBSR can significantly reduce anxiety and improve overall well-being.

Meditation Techniques: Different types of meditation, such as guided imagery, loving-kindness meditation, and transcendental meditation, can help reduce anxiety by promoting relaxation and altering the brain's response to stress. Regular meditation practice can decrease the activity in the brain's default mode network, which is associated with self-referential and anxious thinking.

Pharmacotherapy

Medications can be an important part of the treatment plan for anxiety disorders, particularly for those with severe symptoms.

Selective Serotonin Reuptake Inhibitors (SSRIs): SSRIs, such as fluoxetine (Prozac) and sertraline (Zoloft), are commonly prescribed for anxiety. They work by increasing the levels of serotonin in the brain, which can improve mood and reduce anxiety.

Benzodiazepines: Medications like diazepam (Valium) and alprazolam (Xanax) can be effective for short-term relief of severe anxiety symptoms. However, they can be habit-forming and are generally not recommended for long-term use due to the risk of dependence and withdrawal symptoms.

Beta-Blockers: Beta-blockers, such as propranolol, are sometimes used to manage the physical symptoms of anxiety, such as rapid heartbeat and trembling, especially in situations like performance anxiety.

Lifestyle Changes

Adopting a healthy lifestyle can have a significant impact on anxiety levels. Simple changes can make a big difference in managing symptoms.

Regular Exercise: Physical activity has been shown to reduce anxiety and improve mood. Exercise releases endorphins, which are natural stress relievers. Activities like running, swimming, or yoga can be particularly beneficial.

Healthy Diet: A balanced diet can influence anxiety. Reducing caffeine and sugar intake and incorporating foods rich in omega-3 fatty acids, magnesium, and B vitamins can help manage anxiety symptoms. Staying hydrated and eating regular, balanced meals support overall mental health.

Adequate Sleep: Good sleep hygiene is essential for managing anxiety. Establishing a regular sleep schedule, creating a restful environment, and avoiding screens before bedtime can improve sleep quality and reduce anxiety.

Alternative Therapies

Alternative therapies can complement traditional treatments and offer additional ways to manage anxiety.

Acupuncture: Acupuncture involves inserting thin needles into specific points on the body. Some studies suggest it can help reduce anxiety by promoting relaxation and altering brain chemistry.

Aromatherapy: The use of essential oils, such as lavender and chamomile, can have calming effects and reduce anxiety. Aromatherapy can be practiced through diffusers, topical application, or baths.

Biofeedback: Biofeedback teaches individuals to control physiological functions such as heart rate and muscle tension through feedback from sensors. By learning to control these functions, individuals can reduce anxiety symptoms.

Support Systems and Community Resources

Having a strong support system and access to community resources can significantly aid in managing anxiety.

Support Groups: Support groups provide a space for individuals to share their experiences and receive encouragement from others who understand what they are going through. Groups can be found in person or online and can be specific to certain types of anxiety disorders.

Therapists and Counselors: Professional therapists and counselors can offer personalized guidance and support. They can

Part 7: The Digital Age

This chapter emphasizes the power of collective resources and relationships in providing emotional, psychological, and practical support. Understanding and leveraging these systems can significantly enhance the well-being of individuals struggling with anxiety.

The vast growth and utilization of technology has transformed humanity in unseen ways. The Digital Age, a period following the Information Age, has engendered a multitude of changes to our societal structure as a result of the Internet, advances in computer technology, and the progressive digitalization of our everyday interactions. Each generation learns and experiences life in different ways during this era. This study will focus on Generation Z, the current youngest generation, which had their formative years comprise their entire understanding of and exposure to the digital landscape. Researchers, writers, and professionals in education, psychology, and business commonly refer to this generation as the "Anxious Generation." The present study aims to add a specific specification to the scholarly work that explores the lives of Generation Z.

In reviewing the current research about Generation Z in the Information Communication and Technology (ICT) academic literature, it became evident that many studies focused on how Gen Z students use technology in an educational setting. Most studies concentrate on comparing how Generation Z differs in how they use technology in comparison to previous Generation Y students, often referred to as "Millennials." Although the research studies do provide valuable insights, very few studies focused solely on students' well-being and their anxiety levels in this young digital age generation. Addressing the previously mentioned issue in the literature, the objective of this study was to explore the relationship between psychological well-being and life satisfaction in Generation Z students, through the influencing factor of perceived stress within an academic context.

Importance of Social Support

Social support is a cornerstone in the management of anxiety. It involves the perception and reality that one is cared for, has assistance available from other people, and is part of a supportive social network.

Buffering Effect: Social support acts as a buffer against the effects of stress. Knowing that one has a supportive network can reduce the perceived threat of stressful situations and provide emotional comfort.

Emotional and Practical Support: Emotional support includes empathy, love, trust, and caring from others, which can help alleviate feelings of loneliness and isolation. Practical support includes tangible assistance, such as help with tasks and financial aid, which can reduce anxiety related to daily challenges.

Family and Friends

Family and friends are often the first line of defense against anxiety. Their support can be instrumental in managing symptoms and providing a sense of belonging.

Communication: Open and honest communication with family and friends about anxiety can foster understanding and support. Sharing experiences and feelings can help reduce the stigma associated with anxiety and make it easier to seek help.

Involvement in Treatment: Family members and friends can be involved in the treatment process by attending therapy sessions, helping with treatment adherence, and providing encouragement. This involvement can enhance the effectiveness of treatment and provide a broader support network.

Building a Supportive Environment: Creating a supportive home environment that reduces stressors and promotes relaxation can help manage anxiety. This might include establishing routines, reducing clutter, and promoting healthy lifestyle habits.

Support Groups

Support groups offer a structured environment where individuals with similar experiences can share their stories and provide mutual support.

Peer Support: Support groups provide a platform for individuals to connect with others who understand their struggles. This peer support can be incredibly validating and empowering.

Group Therapy: Group therapy, led by a trained facilitator, can offer additional therapeutic benefits. It combines the elements of traditional therapy with the support of peers, providing a safe space for individuals to explore their anxiety and learn from others.

Specialized Groups: There are support groups tailored to specific types of anxiety disorders, such as social anxiety, panic disorder, and generalized anxiety disorder. These specialized groups can provide more targeted support and resources.

Workplace Support

The workplace is a significant source of stress for many individuals, making workplace support crucial for managing anxiety.

Mental Health Policies: Implementing mental health policies that promote a supportive work environment can help reduce workplace anxiety. This includes policies on work-life balance, stress management programs, and access to mental health resources.

Employee Assistance Programs (EAPs): EAPs provide employees with access to counseling and mental health services. These programs can offer confidential support for anxiety and other mental health issues, helping employees manage their symptoms while maintaining productivity.

Supportive Leadership: Leadership that prioritizes mental health and fosters an open dialogue about anxiety can create a more inclusive and supportive workplace. Managers trained in mental health awareness can better support their teams and reduce workplace stressors.

Online Communities

Online communities provide a convenient and accessible platform for support, especially for those who may not have access to local resources or prefer the anonymity of online interactions.

Forums and Social Media: Online forums and social media groups allow individuals to share their experiences, ask questions, and offer support to others. These platforms can provide a sense of community and reduce feelings of isolation.

Virtual Support Groups: Virtual support groups offer the same benefits as in-person groups but with added convenience. These groups can be especially helpful for those with mobility issues or those living in remote areas.

Mental Health Apps: There are numerous apps designed to help manage anxiety, offering features like guided meditation, mood tracking, and virtual therapy sessions. These tools can complement traditional treatment methods and provide additional support.

Role of Mental Health Professionals

Mental health professionals play a vital role in providing support and treatment for anxiety.

Therapists and Counselors: Licensed therapists and counselors can offer personalized treatment plans, including CBT, DBT, and other therapeutic approaches. Regular sessions with a mental health professional can help individuals develop coping strategies and address underlying issues.

Psychiatrists: Psychiatrists can provide medication management for anxiety disorders. They can work with patients to find the most effective medication and dosage, monitor progress, and adjust treatment as needed.

Integration with Community Support: Mental health professionals can help individuals integrate community and social support into their treatment plans, ensuring a holistic approach to managing anxiety. They can provide referrals to support groups, community resources, and other forms of assistance.

Part 8: Coping Mechanisms and Strategies

In the past few years, we've witnessed an overwhelming increase in anxiety among college students. Indeed, anxiety has now become the most common concern in college students, surpassing even depression. There does not appear to be a simple explanation for the divergence. Research shows that college students in this generation, born between 1982 and 2002, may be more anxious than their predecessors. Data from two large population-based surveys of US colleges show that the amount of anxiety and concern for students has been steadily rising since similar data were first reported in 1985. This trend has been linked with the new generation's prioritization of goals that are linked to extrinsic success, wealth, and fame, and the value placed on schooling as a way to achieve that success, suggesting that anxiety is a reaction to external pressures. However, research has also shown that there are no significant differences between current college students' desire for money and their weaker work ethos and whining behavior relative to Keniston's "not-yet-broken-in" generation that followed the youth of the 1960s. For now, research is unable to explain the increase.

This focuses on various coping mechanisms and strategies that individuals can use to manage anxiety effectively. These techniques range from immediate, short-term solutions to long-term lifestyle changes. The goal is to provide a comprehensive toolkit that individuals can draw from to find what works best for their

unique situations.

Key Points

1. **Immediate Coping Strategies**
2. **Cognitive Techniques**
3. **Behavioral Strategies**
4. **Emotional Regulation**
5. **Lifestyle Modifications**
6. **Social Support and Communication**
7. **Professional Help and Therapy**

Immediate Coping Strategies

Immediate coping strategies are techniques that can provide quick relief from acute anxiety symptoms. These methods can be employed in moments of high stress to regain control and calm down.

Deep Breathing: Deep breathing exercises, such as diaphragmatic breathing or the 4-7-8 technique, help activate the body's relaxation response. Focusing on slow, deep breaths can reduce the physical symptoms of anxiety, such as rapid heartbeat and shallow breathing.

Progressive Muscle Relaxation (PMR): PMR involves tensing and then slowly releasing each muscle group in the body. This technique can reduce muscle tension and promote physical relaxation, which in turn helps alleviate anxiety.

Grounding Techniques: Grounding techniques, such as the 5-4-3-2-1 method (naming five things you can see, four you can touch, three you can hear, two you can smell, and one you can taste), help divert attention from anxiety-provoking thoughts to the present moment. This can be particularly effective during panic attacks or moments of intense anxiety.

Cognitive Techniques

Cognitive techniques focus on changing the thought patterns that contribute to anxiety. By addressing cognitive distortions and irrational beliefs, individuals can reduce their anxiety levels.

Cognitive Restructuring: This involves identifying negative thought patterns and challenging them with evidence-based reasoning. For example, replacing catastrophic thinking ("I'm going to fail completely") with more balanced thoughts ("I have prepared well and will do my best").

Mindfulness-Based Cognitive Therapy (MBCT): MBCT combines traditional cognitive therapy with mindfulness practices. It helps individuals become more aware of their thoughts and feelings without getting caught up in them. This awareness allows for more deliberate responses to anxiety-provoking situations rather than automatic reactions.

Acceptance and Commitment Therapy (ACT): ACT encourages individuals to accept their anxiety rather than fight it and to commit to actions that align with their values despite their anxiety. This approach helps reduce the struggle against anxiety and promotes a more meaningful life.

Behavioral Strategies

Behavioral strategies involve changing behaviors to reduce anxiety and improve coping skills.

Exposure Therapy: Gradual exposure to feared situations or stimuli can help desensitize individuals to their anxiety triggers. Over time, repeated exposure can reduce the intensity of the anxiety response.

Activity Scheduling: Planning and engaging in positive activities can provide structure and distract from anxious thoughts. Scheduling enjoyable activities can also boost mood and provide a sense of accomplishment.

Behavioral Activation: This technique encourages individuals to engage in activities they have been avoiding due to anxiety. By gradually increasing participation in these activities, individuals can break the cycle of avoidance and improve their mood.

Emotional Regulation

Emotional regulation involves managing and responding to emotional experiences in healthy ways.

Emotion Regulation Skills: Techniques such as identifying and labeling emotions, practicing self-compassion, and using positive affirmations can help manage emotional responses to anxiety. Developing these skills can lead to a better understanding and control of emotional reactions.

Distress Tolerance: Distress tolerance skills, such as using distraction, self-soothing, and radical acceptance, help individuals cope with high levels of emotional distress. These skills are particularly useful during intense episodes of anxiety.

Interpersonal Effectiveness: Improving communication skills and assertiveness can help manage anxiety in social interactions. Learning to set boundaries, express needs clearly, and resolve conflicts effectively can reduce social anxiety.

Lifestyle Modifications

Long-term lifestyle changes can have a significant impact on anxiety management.

Regular Exercise: Physical activity releases endorphins, which are natural mood enhancers. Regular exercise can reduce anxiety levels, improve sleep, and boost overall well-being. Activities like running, swimming, yoga, and tai chi are particularly beneficial.

Healthy Diet: Nutrition plays a role in mental health. A balanced diet rich in omega-3 fatty acids, magnesium, and vitamins B and D can support brain health and reduce anxiety symptoms. Avoiding caffeine, alcohol, and sugar can also help manage anxiety.

Adequate Sleep: Good sleep hygiene, such as maintaining a regular sleep schedule, creating a restful sleep environment, and avoiding screens before bedtime, is essential for reducing anxiety. Adequate sleep can improve mood, cognitive function, and overall resilience to stress.

Social Support and Communication

Building and maintaining strong social connections can provide emotional support and reduce feelings of isolation.

Building a Support Network: Developing relationships with family, friends, and peers who offer understanding and support is crucial. Being able to talk about anxiety and share experiences can provide relief and perspective.

Effective Communication: Learning to communicate feelings and needs assertively can help reduce anxiety in interpersonal relationships. Clear and honest communication can prevent misunderstandings and reduce social stress.

Joining Support Groups: Participating in support groups, whether in-person or online, can provide a sense of community and shared experience. Support groups offer a platform to discuss challenges, share coping strategies, and receive encouragement from others facing similar issues.

Professional Help and Therapy

Professional intervention is often necessary for managing more severe or persistent anxiety.

Individual Therapy: One-on-one therapy with a licensed mental health professional can provide personalized treatment plans and support. Therapists can help individuals explore the underlying causes of their anxiety and develop effective coping strategies.

Group Therapy: Group therapy offers the benefits of individual therapy within a group setting. Participants can learn from each other's experiences and gain insights into their own anxiety through group dynamics and discussions.

Medication: Medications, such as SSRIs, benzodiazepines, and beta-blockers, can be effective in managing anxiety symptoms. A psychiatrist can prescribe and monitor medication, adjusting treatment as needed to find the most effective approach.

Part 9: The Role of Community and Support Systems

Anxiety is an inherent human emotion that plays a multifaceted role in a person's daily life. The emotional reaction of anxiety itself ensures the probable presence of a threat in the social and ecological environment. Due to anxiety, one remains on high alert and is prepared for any threats that may occur. The modern generation appears to be the most anxious members of society based on their worsening mental and emotional health, a rise in the number of lifestyle-related diseases, and the high levels of stress they face in global complex societies. Globalization, advances in technology, rapid communication, and inadequate time to reflect have provided a significant impact on what appears to be the growing anxious population.

The possible increase in the prevalence of anxiety is the result of the inability to manage fast changes in society, stress related to job performance, and increased complex social interactions in a diverse group of individuals with different cultural backgrounds.

To alleviate these issues, community members and support groups are active in their roles of providing emotional, physical, social, and mental support, which are essential for the well-being of the anxious generation.

In this paper, we define the notion of entrepreneurial society and address theoretical links between entrepreneurship, anxiety-associated factors, anxiety behavioral controls, and an understanding of emotional well-being. We also acknowledge the essential role of the community in being a support system for the anxious generation while building and leveraging a support structure.

Such a support structure involves family, friends, educational institutions, alternative support groups, mental health professionals, and societal influencers. In this paper, we focus on understanding the role of community support themselves to alleviate the anxiety in the entrepreneurial society.

The significance of the community is threefold: as primary and secondary individual emotional supporters to alleviate uneasiness, through community entrepreneurship as a means for cognitive and emotional employment, and by community support as a base to prevent and treat anomalous anxiety.

The Power of Social Connections

Social connections are fundamental to human well-being. They provide a sense of belonging, reduce feelings of isolation, and offer emotional support. For individuals with anxiety, strong social connections can act as a buffer against stress and help in coping with challenging situations.

Emotional Support: Close relationships with family and friends can provide emotional support, which is essential for mental health. Knowing that there are people who care and are willing to listen can significantly reduce feelings of anxiety and loneliness.

Sense of Belonging: Being part of a community or social group provides a sense of belonging. This connection can enhance self-esteem and reduce feelings of alienation, which are often associated with anxiety.

Shared Experiences: Sharing experiences with others who understand what it's like to live with anxiety can be incredibly validating. It helps individuals feel understood and less alone in their struggles.

Family Support

Family can be a primary source of support for individuals dealing with anxiety. The role of family in providing stability, understanding, and encouragement is invaluable.

Open Communication: Encouraging open and honest communication within the family can help individuals express their feelings and needs. Family members who are aware of the anxiety can offer better support and avoid actions that may exacerbate the condition.

Creating a Safe Environment: Families can create a safe and supportive home environment by reducing stressors and promoting healthy routines. This includes respecting boundaries, providing reassurance, and fostering a calm and nurturing atmosphere.

Involvement in Treatment: Family members can play a role in treatment by attending therapy sessions, supporting treatment plans, and encouraging adherence to medication or therapy regimens. Their involvement can enhance the effectiveness of treatment.

Friendship Networks

Friendships provide another layer of support outside of the family. Friends can offer a different perspective, engage in shared activities, and provide companionship.

Social Activities: Engaging in social activities with friends can distract from anxious thoughts and promote positive experiences. Regular social interactions can improve mood and reduce feelings of isolation.

Peer Support: Friends who are also dealing with anxiety or who understand mental health challenges can provide peer support.

They can share coping strategies, offer empathy, and provide a sense of solidarity.

Non-Judgmental Listening: Having friends who listen without judgment can be incredibly comforting. Knowing there is someone to talk to during difficult times can alleviate anxiety and provide emotional relief.

Community Organizations

Community organizations, including religious groups, non-profits, and local clubs, offer additional resources and support networks.

Access to Resources: Community organizations often provide access to resources such as counseling services, support groups, and educational workshops. These resources can offer practical assistance and information on managing anxiety.

Sense of Community: Being part of a community organization can provide a sense of purpose and belonging. Participation in group activities and events fosters social connections and reduces feelings of isolation.

Volunteer Opportunities: Volunteering for community organizations can provide a sense of fulfillment and reduce anxiety. Helping others can shift focus away from personal anxieties and promote positive emotions.

Support Groups

Support groups offer a structured environment where individuals with similar experiences can share their stories and provide mutual support.

Group Therapy: Group therapy, led by a trained facilitator, combines therapeutic techniques with peer support. Participants can learn from each other, gain insights, and practice new coping strategies in a safe environment.

Peer Support Groups: Peer support groups, whether in-person or online, provide a platform for individuals to connect, share experiences, and offer encouragement. These groups can reduce feelings of isolation and provide practical advice from others who understand the challenges of living with anxiety.

Specialized Groups: There are support groups tailored to specific types of anxiety, such as social anxiety, panic disorder, or PTSD. Specialized groups offer more targeted support and resources.

Online Communities

The digital age has enabled the creation of online communities that provide support and resources for individuals with anxiety.

Forums and Social Media: Online forums and social media groups allow individuals to share their experiences, ask questions, and offer support to others. These platforms can provide a sense of community and reduce feelings of isolation, especially for those who may not have access to local support groups.

Virtual Support Groups: Virtual support groups offer the same benefits as in-person groups but with added convenience. They can be particularly helpful for individuals with mobility issues, those living in remote areas, or those who prefer the anonymity of online interactions.

Mental Health Apps: There are numerous apps designed to help manage anxiety.

These apps offer features like guided meditation, mood tracking, and virtual therapy sessions. They can complement traditional treatment methods and provide additional support.

Professional Support Systems

Professional support systems, including therapists, counselors, and mental health organizations, play a crucial role in managing anxiety.

Therapists and Counselors: Licensed therapists and counselors provide individualized treatment plans and support.

Regular sessions with a mental health professional can help individuals develop coping strategies, address underlying issues, and monitor progress.

Psychiatrists: Psychiatrists can prescribe and manage medication for anxiety disorders. They work with patients to find the most effective medication and dosage, adjust treatment as needed, and monitor side effects.

Mental Health Organizations: Organizations like the Anxiety and Depression Association of America

(ADAA) and the National Alliance on Mental Illness (NAMI) offer resources, support groups, and educational programs. These organizations provide valuable information and support for individuals and families dealing with anxiety.

Acknowledgements

Creating "The Anxious Generation" has been a deeply rewarding journey, and I am grateful to many individuals and groups whose contributions have been invaluable.

First and foremost, I would like to thank all the individuals who bravely shared their personal stories and testimonials. Your honesty and vulnerability provide the heart and soul of this book. Your experiences will undoubtedly offer comfort and hope to many readers.

I am deeply grateful to the mental health professionals who have guided me and countless others through the complexities of anxiety. Your expertise, dedication, and compassion are truly transformative. Special thanks to my therapist, whose insights and support have been instrumental in my own journey.

Thank you to the numerous support groups and online communities that foster understanding and solidarity among those dealing with anxiety. Your work in creating safe spaces for sharing and healing is profoundly impactful.

I would also like to acknowledge the role of community organizations and mental health advocacy groups. Your tireless efforts in raising awareness, providing resources, and advocating for better mental health care are making a significant difference in the lives of many.

A heartfelt thanks to my editor and publishing team for your guidance, expertise, and belief in this project. Your dedication to bringing this book to life is deeply appreciated.

Finally, to the readers of this book: thank you for taking the time to explore "The Anxious Generation." It is my hope that you find comfort, understanding, and practical strategies within these pages.

Remember, you are not alone, and there is a community of support available to you.

God bless you all.

THANKS FOR READING